I'll Tell What I Saw

Images from
Dante's *Divine Comedy*

MICHAEL MAZUR

With Passages Translated by

ROBERT PINSKY

SARABANDE BOOKS
LOUISVILLE, KENTUCKY

FIRST EDITION

Managing Editor
Sarabande Books, Inc.
2234 Dundee Road, Suite 200
Louisville, KY 40205

Library of Congress Cataloging-in-Publication Data

Dante Alighieri, 1265–1321.
  [Divina commedia. English. Selections.]
  I'll tell what I saw : selections from Dante's Divine comedy : illustrations by Michael Mazur ;
translations from the Italian by Robert Pinsky. — 1st ed.
      p. cm.
  ISBN 978-1-932511-77-2 (pbk. : alk. paper)
  I. Pinsky, Robert. II. Mazur, Michael, 1935– III. Title.
  PQ4315.15.P56 2009
  851'.1—dc22
                        2009020295

ISBN-13: 978-1-932511-78-9

Cover design by Michael Mazur.
Interior and text design by Kirkby Gann Tittle.

Manufactured in the Canada.
This book is printed on acid-free paper.

Sarabande Books is a nonprofit literary organization.

The Kentucky Arts Council, the state arts agency, supports Sarabande Books with state tax dollars and federal funding from the National Endowment for the Arts.

LIST OF ILLUSTRATIONS

Frontispiece: Canto 1, Etching and Aquatint with coloring, 1997, for the portfolio *The Inferno of Dante*, 41 etchings, 2000.

Inferno, Canto 1: "La Selva Oscura / The Dark Wood." Watercolor study for *The Inferno of Dante*, Farrar, Straus, & Giroux, 1994.

Inferno, Canto I: "The Illusive Hill." Watercolor study for *The Inferno of Dante*, Farrar, Straus & Giroux, 1994.

Inferno, Canto III: "Charonte / Charon (The Boatman)." Watercolor study for *The Inferno of Dante*, Farrar, Straus & Giroux, 1994.

Inferno, Canto V: "I lussieri / The Lustful." Watercolor study for *The Inferno of Dante*, Farrar, Straus & Giroux, 1994.

Inferno, Canto V: "Paolo e Francesca / Paola and Francesca." Montage of etching and monotype, 1990s–2000.

Inferno, Canto XI: "Plan of the Inferno." Etching and digital print, 2008.

Inferno, Canto XIII: "I suicidi / The suicides." Etching from *The Inferno of Dante*, Farrar, Straus & Giroux, 2000.

Inferno, Canto XXI: "I Barratieri / The Barrators (Swindlers)." Ink-jet manipulation of color etching used for the cover of *The Inferno of Dante* (Farrar, Straus & Giroux), and digital portfolio of broadsides "Ill Tell What I Saw," 2008.

Inferno, Canto XXXIV: "DIS (Lucifer)." Etching and aquatint for *The Inferno of Dante*, Farrar, Straus & Giroux, 2000.

Inferno, Canto XXXIV: "a reveder le stelle / To see the stars again." Etching and aquatint for portfolio for *The Inferno of Dante* (Farrar, Straus & Giroux, 2000), and the portfolio of broadsides "I'll tell What I Saw," 2008.

Purgatory, Canto I: "The arrival." Inkjet print, 2007.

Purgatory, Canto II: "The Angelic Ferry." Inkjet print, 2008.

Purgatory, Canto X: "The Steps." Inkjet print, 2007–8.

Purgatory, Canto XXVII: "The Cleansing Fire." Monotype of "The Chase" from the 1980s, modified by photoshop, 2008.

Purgatory, Canto XXX: Various elements from paintings and the web, modified in Photoshop, 2007–8.

Purgatory, "The map of Purgatory." Inkjet print, 2008.

Paradise, Canto 1: "Leaving Purgatory." Inkjet print, 2008.

Paradise, Canto I: "The Journey." Inkjet print, 2008.

Paradise, Canto X: "The Heaven of the Sun." Inkjet version of a painting from 2007.

Paradise, Canto XII: "The Rose." Inkjet print, 2008.

Paradise, Canto XXXIII: From the Last Canto of *Paradise*, Inkjet print, 2008.

PREFACE

VISION CAN ATTAIN IMMEASURABLE DEPTH, even on paper surfaces, as Michael Mazur's works in this book demonstrate.

Mazur has been reading Dante's *Commedia* in Italian for many decades—reading it, in my experience, almost constantly. When I was working on my translation of the *Inferno*, with Michael a few miles away working on his great monotype illustrations for that book, I gained immensely from what I consider a collaboration. Beyond valuable consultation about particular phrases or passages, Michael Mazur's approach to the *Inferno* gave me inspiration and guidance in understanding Dante. The *Inferno* monotypes, nourished by the artist's intense engagement with the poetry, are themselves acts of translation, embodying certain vital principles.

Mazur decided from the outset never to show Dante and Virgil—but rather what they see, emphasizing immediacy, freshly imagined. The Mazur images present themselves as perceived through the pilgrim Dante's eyes and sensibility—not the diorama or stage-like tableau with two figures in the foreground, as in the familiar Gustave Doré plates. In another kind of immediacy and conviction, Mazur declines the superficially appealing cliché of contemporary visual references. The temptation to suggest (for example) the faces of American public figures, buildings, brand-names, or artifacts invites a facile irony. And it is absolute conviction, not irony, that gives the *Commedia* its propulsive energy.

Entering Dante's creation entirely, not standing outside it, nor in a modern world apart from it, enables Mazur to imagine the poetry's images with a tremendous, radical freshness, stemming from a lifelong passion. When he was an undergraduate, Mazur took time off to live in Florence and pursue art full-time: a test of his calling. Reading Dante in Dante's city, he conceived a series of *Inferno* illustrations as his senior thesis—a project Mazur's adviser counseled him was far too ambitious. (He illustrated Oscar Wilde's *Salome* instead.) Later, during the Vietnam War, he considered a series of anti-war *Inferno* illustrations, going so far as making some remarkable studies.

In 1992, Michael attended a poetry reading where I read some of the first cantos of my translation. Immediately after the reading, he told me (in his animated manner) that whether I wanted it or not, whether Farrar, Straus and Giroux would want it or not, he was going to make a series of monotype, black-and-white illustrations. That same evening, he conceived what became the design of *The Inferno of Dante* as FSG published it a couple of years later: the text of the Italian original on the left-hand (verso) pages, the English on the right (recto), and at the beginning of every canto a full-page illustration on the verso page and a Roman numeral, with a caption of a few lines, on the recto. The next morning, Mazur went to work, and that afternoon he showed me the first images that after much work evolved into the book illustrations.

A monotype, as I became vividly aware, is a unique impression pressed onto a sheet of paper from an inked plate. In Mazur's mastery of the medium, the black ink of the *Inferno* illustrations can look like ice or water or earth or skin or fire or cloth or masonry or air. Squeezed through the press, each monotype incorporates the unique, unpredictable results of pressure, along with the intentions of the artist. In black and white, with forms and textures marrying chance to expertise, the monotypes convey the variety of earthly life and of Dante's underworld within the stringent means—the earthly materials and forces—of their medium.

After our *Inferno* project was completed, I can remember Michael speculating about the colorist or the geometrical artist who might suitably undertake illustrations for a *Purgatorio* and a *Paradiso*: in some pictorial medium less strictly earthbound than black ink. And all the time, of course, Michael continued reading and re-reading Dante's poem and thinking about its meanings.

For his new, astonishing color illustrations reproduced in this book, Michael found an equally new, less earthly, and in a way disembodied medium: digital technology. The set of color broadside sheets he produced have an intensity quite different from that of the black-and-white monotypes: equally urgent, but with a transformative freedom and a sometimes ethereal quality of imagination.

As Mazur has described it, he needed a new vocabulary of color: Purgatory expressed by the colors of the earth, and Paradise by ecstatic or even hallucinatory colors. Digital means enabled him to create these ranges of color. The *Inferno* presented a different problem; the original book illustrations used black and white to present a place without sunlight. The colors for these new images of Hell attain an other-worldly feeling opposite to that of the *Paradiso*, the shades and intensities and saturations of the world transformed away from sunlight, into the underworld.

When Michael asked me to provide captions for the *Purgatorio* and *Paradiso* broadside images, I recognized an assignment different in kind, as well as scale, from a full-scale translation like *The Inferno of Dante*. Unlike the *Inferno* captions, extracted from a larger whole, the new brief passages for these broadsides were created specifically for particular images. The assigned passages were chosen by the artist; they translate the specific lines of Dante's Italian that inspired each image. Thus, there was less emphasis on devising a sustained idiom—a poetic medium that could be extended over the variety and expanse of many cantos—than on making an accurate, graceful version of each passage, for each remarkable image.

This book based on those images, like the boxed set of originals, includes along with the brief captions my poem "From the Last Canto of Paradise"—made of lines taken from *Paradiso* XXXIII. It is an honor, and deeply gratifying, to contribute to Michael Mazur's project: gorgeous images that profoundly meditate Dante's *Commedia*.

Robert Pinsky

Inferno

Prologue

by Robert Pinsky
—*For a stage presentation of the* Inferno

To go into it: in the declivity

At the center of Hell

Furthest from the light,

Knotted in ice the Beast himself weeping.

Misery of cold, treachery of dark, agony

Of sin, bottomless sorrow of evil:

Not punishment, but the agony of rage unspent.

To go into it: sorrow of revenge

Never sufficient, extravagant.

Bottomless agony of the self-wounded

Soul in self-extinction

Treacherous soul.

To go into it

The pilgrim becomes the voice of the sinners.

The reader's voice becomes the pilgrim's

As the pilgrim becomes the writer.

To go into it—grappling at the ice-matted

Flank of the Beast, to bring

Sorrow to light.

Unreadable

Body of losses.

To go into it and through it

Or to go into it and never
Through it.

Withdrawal from the world of light.

To go into it to go through it: agony
Of despair, hand in the dark
Plucking at the knot that
The same hand tied
In the light.

INFERNO I *1–10*

Midway on our life's journey, I found myself
    In dark woods, the right road lost. To tell
    About those woods is hard—so tangled and rough

And savage that thinking of it now, I feel
    The old fear stirring: death is hardly more bitter.
    And yet, to treat the good I found there as well

I'll tell what I saw, though how I came to enter
    I cannot well say, being so full of sleep
    Whatever moment it was I began to blunder

Off the true path.

INFERNO I *10–21*

But when I came to stop
Below a hill that marked one end of the valley
That had pierced my heart with terror, I looked up

Toward the crest and saw its shoulders already
Manteled in rays of that bright planet that shows
The road to everyone, whatever our journey.

Then I could feel the terror begin to ease
That churned in my heart's lake all through the night.
As one still panting, ashore from dangerous seas,

Looks back at the deep he has escaped, my thought
Returned, still fleeing, to regard that grim defile
That never left any alive who stayed in it.

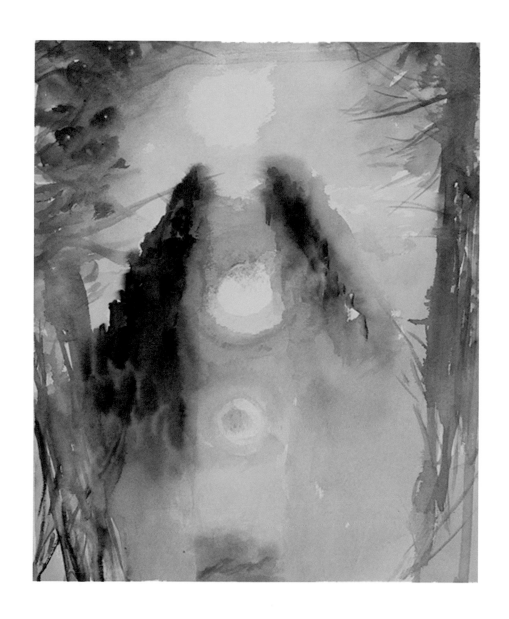

INFERNO III   *70–87*

Then, at the river—an old man in a boat:

    White-haired, as he drew closer shouting at us,

    "Woe to you, wicked souls! Give up the thought

Of Heaven! I come to ferry you across

    Into eternal dark on the opposite side,

    Into fire and ice!"

INFERNO IV 25–45

Here we encountered

No laments that we could hear—except for sighs

That trembled the timeless air: they emanated

From the shadowy sadnesses, not agonies,

Of multitudes of children and women and men.

He said, "And don't you ask, what spirits are these?

Before you go on, I tell you: they did not sin;

If they have merit, it can't suffice without

Baptism, portal to the faith you maintain.

Some lived before the Christian faith, so that

They did not worship God aright—and I

Am one of these. Through this, no other fault,

We are lost, afflicted only this one way:

That having no hope, we live in longing." I heard

These words with heartfelt grief that seized on me

Knowing how many worthy souls endured

Suspension in that Limbo.

INFERNO V   *32–44*

Driven as if to land
They reach the ruin: groaning, tears, laments,

And cursing of the power of Heaven. I learned
They suffer here who sinned in carnal things—
Their reason mastered by desire, suborned.

As winter starlings riding on their wings
Form crowded flocks, so spirits dip and veer
Foundering in the wind's rough buffetings,

Upward or downward, driven here and there
With never ease from pain nor hope of rest.
As chanting cranes will form a line in air,

So I saw souls come uttering cries—wind-tossed,
And lofted by the storm. . . .

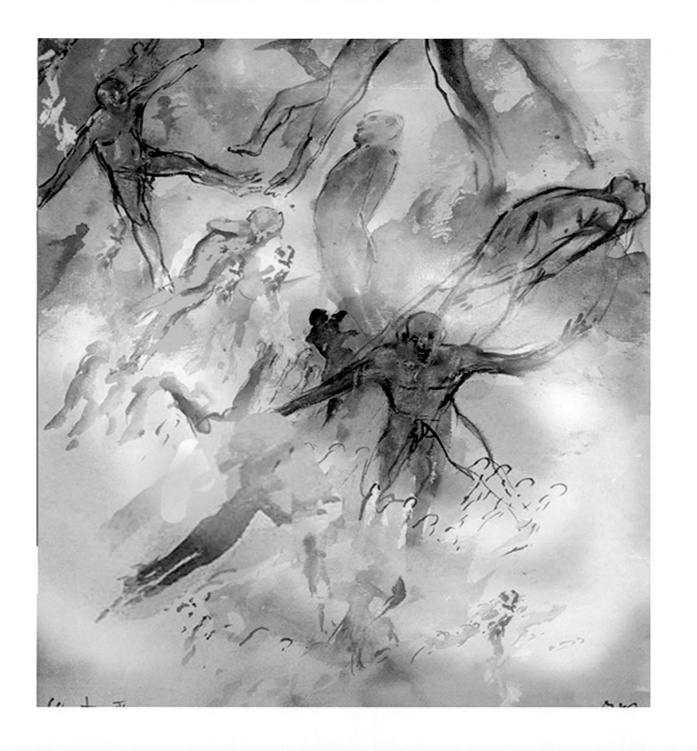

INFERNO V *103–24*

". . . Francesca, your suffering makes me weep

For sorrow and pity—but tell me, in the hours

Of sweetest sighing, how and in what shape

Or manner did love first show you those desires

So hemmed by doubt?" And she to me: "No sadness

Is greater than in misery to rehearse

Memories of joy, as your teacher well can witness.

But if you have so great a craving to measure

Our love's first root, I'll tell it, with the fitness

Of one who weeps and tells. One day, for pleasure,

We read of Lancelot, by love constrained:

Alone, suspecting nothing, at our leisure.

Sometimes at what we read our glances joined,

Looking from the book each to the other's eyes,

And then the color in our faces drained.

But one particular moment alone it was

Defeated us: *the longed-for smile*, it said,

Was kissed by that most noble lover: at this,

This one, who now will never leave my side,

Kissed my mouth, trembling. A Galeotto, that book!

And so was he who wrote it; that day we read

No further."

INFERNO XI *16–27*

                                        "My son,

   Within these rocks three lesser circles fall,

Each one below another, like those you have seen,

   And all of them are packed with accursèd souls;

   In order that hereafter the sight alone

May be sufficient, you will hear what rules

   Determine how and why they are constrained.

   The end of every wickedness that feels

Heaven's hatred is injustice—and each end

   Of this kind, whether by force or fraud, afflicts

   Some other person. But since fraud is found

In humankind as its peculiar vice,

   It angers God more: so the fraudulent

   Are lower, and suffer more unhappiness."

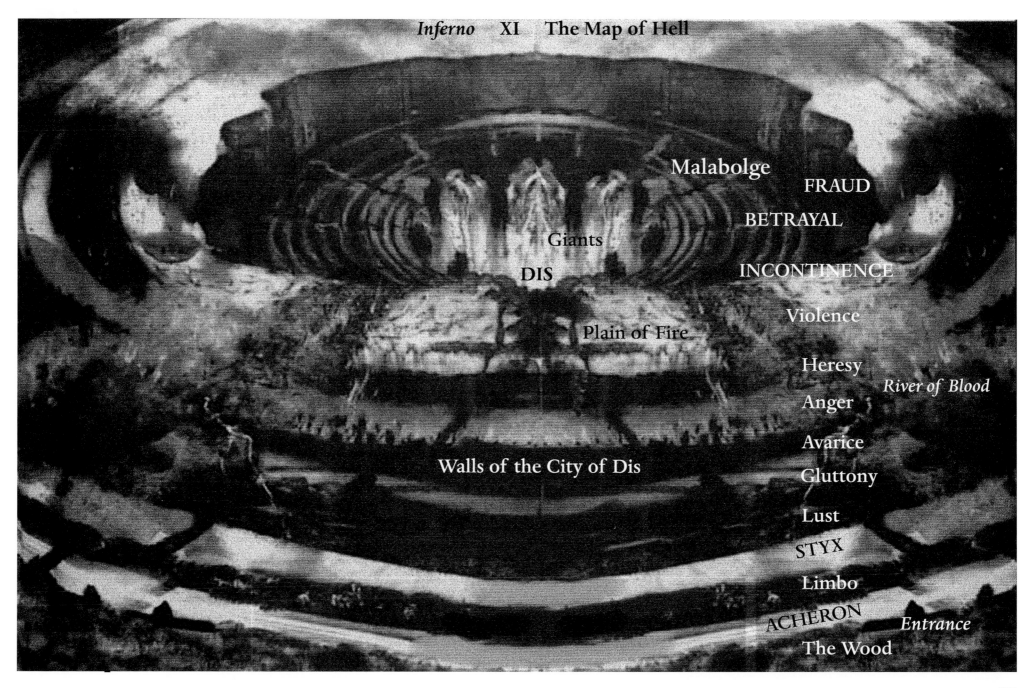

Malabolge

FRAUD

BETRAYAL

Giants

INCONTINENCE

DIS

Violence

Plain of Fire

Heresy

River of Blood

Anger

Avarice

Walls of the City of Dis

Gluttony

Lust

STYX

Limbo

ACHERON

Entrance

The Wood

INFERNO XIII   *88–102*

"When the fierce soul has quit the fleshly case
   It tore itself from, Minos sends it down
   To the seventh depth. It falls to this wooded place—

No chosen spot, but where fortune flings it in—
   And there it sprouts like a grain of spelt, to shoot
   Up as a sapling, then a wild plant: and then

The Harpies, feeding on the foliage, create
   Pain, and an outlet for the pain as well.
   We too shall come like the rest, each one to get

His cast-off body—but not for us to dwell
   Within again, for justice must forbid
   Having what one has robbed oneself of; still,

Here we shall drag them, and through the mournful wood
   Our bodies will be hung: with every one
   Fixed on the thornbush of its wounding shade."

INFERNO XXI   *43–58*

He hurled the sinner down, then turned to rush

    Back down the rocky crag; and no mastiff

    Was ever more impatient to shake the leash

And run his fastest after a fleeing thief.

    The sinner sank below, only to rise

    Rump up—but demons under the bridge's shelf

Cried, "Here's no place to show your Sacred Face!

    You're not out in the Serchio for a swim!

    If you don't want to feel our hooks—like this!—

Then stay beneath the pitch." They struck at him

    With over a hundred hooks, and said, "You'll need

    To dance in secret here—so grab what scam

You're able to, in darkness." They they did

    Just as cooks have their scullions do to steep

    The meat well into the cauldron—with a prod

From their forks keeping it from floating up.

INFERNO XXXIV *31–58*

The emperor of the realm of grief protruded

    From mid-breast up above the surrounding ice.

    A giant's height, and mine, would have provided

Closer comparison than would the size

    Of his arm and a giant. Envision the whole

    That is proportionate to parts like these.

If he was truly once as beautiful

    As he is ugly now, and raised his brows

    Against his Maker—then all sorrow may well

Come out of him. How great a marvel it was

    For me to see three faces on his head:

    In front there was a red one; joined to this,

Each over the midpoint of a shoulder, he had

    Two others—all three joining at the crown.

    That on the right appeared to be a shade

Of whitish yellow; the third had such a mien

    As those who come from where the Nile descends.

    Two wings spread forth from under each face's chin,

Strong, and befitting such a bird, immense—

    I have never seen at sea so broad a sail—

    Unfeathered, batlike, and issuing three winds

That went forth as he beat them, to freeze the whole

    Realm of Cocytus that surrounded him.

    He wept with all six eyes, and the tears fell

Over his three chins mingled with bloody foam.

    The teeth of each mouth held a sinner, kept

    As by a flax rake: thus he held three of them

In agony. . . .

INFERNO XXXIV *128–140*

                        There is below,

As far from Beelzebub as one can be

Within his tomb, a place one cannot know
  By sight, but by the sound a little runnel
  Makes as it wends the hollow rock its flow

Has worn, descending through its winding channel:
  To get back up to the shining world from there
  My guide and I went into that hidden tunnel;

And following its path, we took no care
  To rest, but climbed: he first, then I—so far,
  Through a round aperture I saw appear

Some of the beautiful things that Heaven bears,
Where we came forth, and once more saw the stars.

Purgatorio

PURGATORIO I *13–21*

                                        A tender cast
                  Of oriental sapphire, gathering its light

          Across the sky's calm face, pure to the first
                  Circle, restored my eyes to their delight
                  As soon as I came from where my eyes and chest

          Had suffered dead air. That planet whose fair light
                  Encourages love made all the East sky smile,
                  Veiling the Fish, her escorts.

PURGATORIO II *16–29*

     . . . and then—may I see it again!—a light
  Came skimming the ocean toward us at a speed
  No flight could equal, which, while I glanced from it

For just an instant so I could question my guide,
  Grew brighter and bigger. Then on each side appeared
  A whiteness, and little by little from its underside

Another whiteness. My master said not a word
  Till the first whitenesses appeared as a pair of wings.
  Then, when he saw the pilot clearly, he ordered:

Bend, bend your knees! Behold the angel of God!

PURGATORIO X   *7–16*

Now we were climbing a narrow cleft in the rock,
   Which bent this way and that as it rose and fell
   The way a wave recedes and surges back.

"Here we will have to apply a bit of skill,"
   My guide began, "by keeping close as we can,
   Now here, now there, along whichever wall

Declines away." This method slowed us down,
   Making the progress of our steps so scant
   That the declining orb of the waning moon

Was in bed before we finished our ascent,
At last emerging from that needle's eye.

39

THE EARTHLY PARADISE

LOVE EXCESSIVE

The Lascivious

The Gluttonous

The Avaricious

LOVE DEFECTIVE

The Slothful

LOVE PERVERTED

The Wrathful

The Envious

The Proud

ANTE-PURGATORY

The Excommunicate

The Lethargic

The Unabsolved

Negligent Rulers

PURGATORIO XXVII   *7–27*

. . . The angel stood just outside the flames and sang
"*Beati mundo corde!*" — in a voice more live
Than any in this our life. "The fire must sting,

Before you go any further, blessed souls. Go in,
Enter the fire, don't let yourself be deaf
To the singing just beyond it," he said. And then,

At that, I felt as though thrown into the grave.
Huddled above my hands, I stared at the fire
Recalling burnt bodies I had some memory of,

Until my guides turned toward me. Virgil said, "Here,
My son, there may be torment— but there's no death.
Remember! Remember, when you had so much fear

Mounted on the monster Geryon, I kept you safe—
What will I do now, when we're nearer to God?
Be assured, if you spent a thousand years in the depth

Of that fire's belly, not one hair on your head
Could it singe bald . . .

PURGATORIO XXX   *64–79*

I saw the Lady I had first seen in her veil

At the festival of angels. She turned her eyes

Toward me, from across the water. The cloth that fell

In sheer folds from her crown of Minerva's leaves

Kept me from seeing her face, but I heard her speak—

Regally, in the even tone of one who saves

The most heated words for last. She told me: "Look

Well at my face, be well assured, make sure

I am Beatrice. What made you undertake

To climb that mountain? Was it knowing that here

One is in bliss?" . . . My eyes fell to that clear water

But seeing my own shamed face reflected there,

I looked away, down at the grass, in shame . . .

Paradiso

PARADISO I   *54–63*

I fixed my eyes on the sun—beyond our ways,
There many things are granted to be done

That here are beyond our human faculties,
For that is the Place designed for humankind.
I endured it neither long, nor so short a time

That I couldn't see it burn with an inner fire
As bright as molten iron, so that it seemed
Day had been added to day, as though the power

Of One who could have added a second sun
Had done so, to adorn the heavens.

PARADISO I *38–44*

The world's Lamp rises to mortals at outlet-places

That vary—but takes a better course, conjoined

With better stars, where four circles join three crosses,

And tempers and stamps the world's wax to be more

In its own fashion. Nearly such a rising-point

Had made it be morning there and evening here,

With all that hemisphere white, and this one dark.

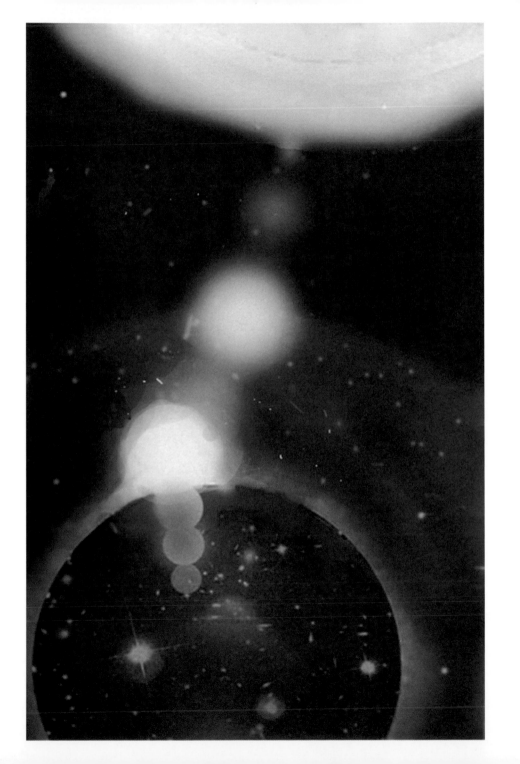

PLAN OF PARADISE: THE TEN HEAVENS

1. Heaven of the Moon : Faithfulness marred by inconsistency

2. Mercury : Service marred by ambition

3. Venus: Love marred by wantoness

4. The Sun: Wisdome; Theologians

5. Mars: Courage; Warriors

6. Jupiter: Justice; Rulers

7. Saturn: Temperance; Contemplatives

8. The Fixed Stars: The Church Triumphant

9. The Crystalline, or Primium Mobile: The Angelic Orders

10. The Empyrean: The Holy Trinity, The Virgin; The Angels and the Saints

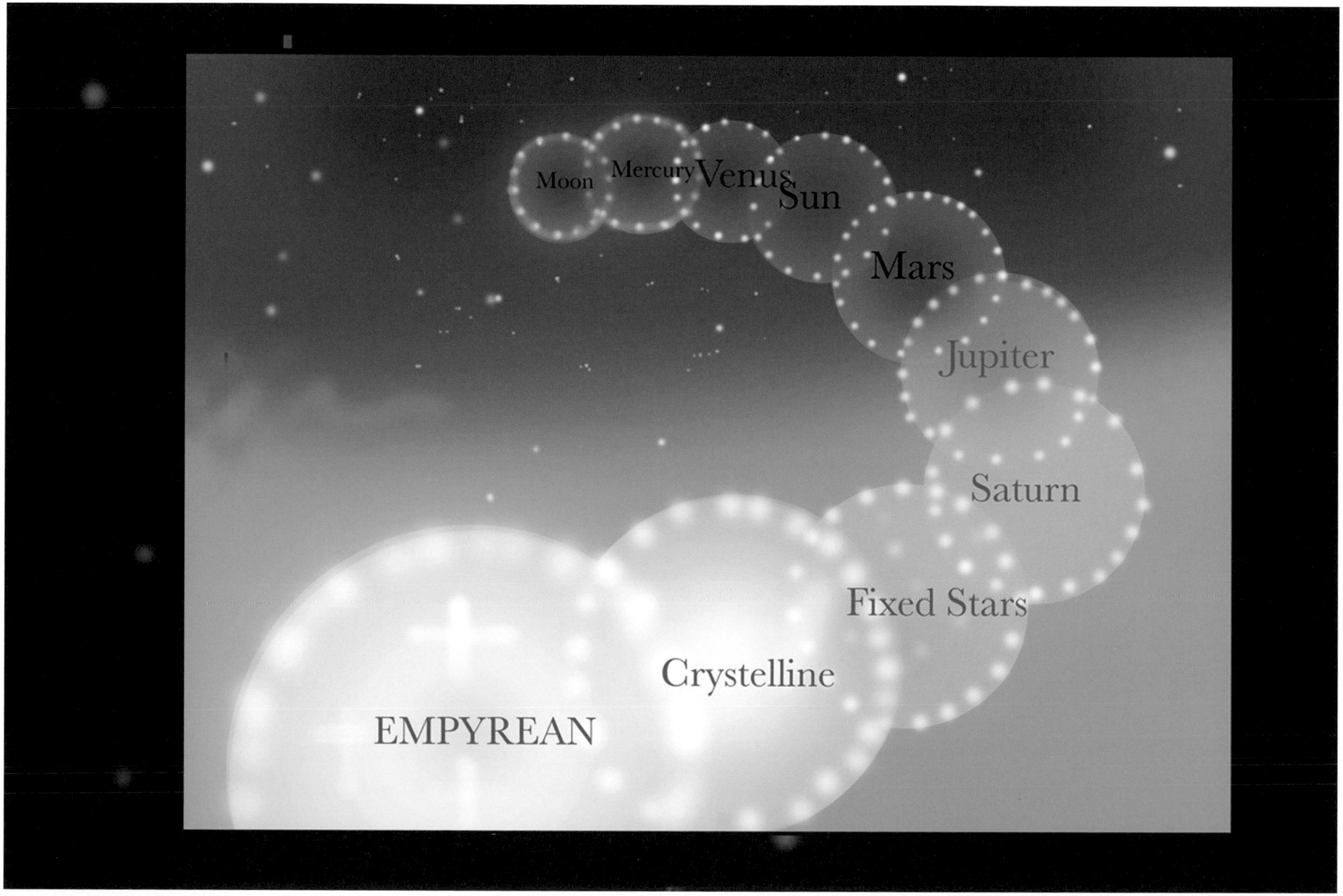
Moon
Mercury
Venus
Sun
Mars
Jupiter
Saturn
Fixed Stars
Crystelline
EMPYREAN

PARADISO X *64–78*

. . . and I saw a multitude of flashing lights,

Vivid and overwhelming. They made us their center

And made a crown of themselves, sweeter in voice

Even than they were brilliant in their splendor,

Encircling the way we sometimes see the Moon,

Latona's daughter, encircled by light when moisture

Imbues night air so the thread that marks her zone

Is held suspended in it. Heaven's court,

From which I have returned, is the domain

Of gems too precious and beautiful for transport

Out of that realm: such was what those lights sang—

Anyone not winged to fly there can await the report

Delivered by one who is mute.

PARADISO XII *1–9, 19–21*

The moment the blessed flame's last word was spoken
The holy millstone began to turn, and before
It had completed the first full revolution

Another wheel enclosed it, and motion for motion,
Song for song, matched it . . . song that by as far
Surpasses our conceptions of muses or sirens—

With such sweet pipes—as an original splendor
Surpasses its reflection. So the two garlands
Of eternal roses encircled us, the further,

Surrounding one responding to the nearer.

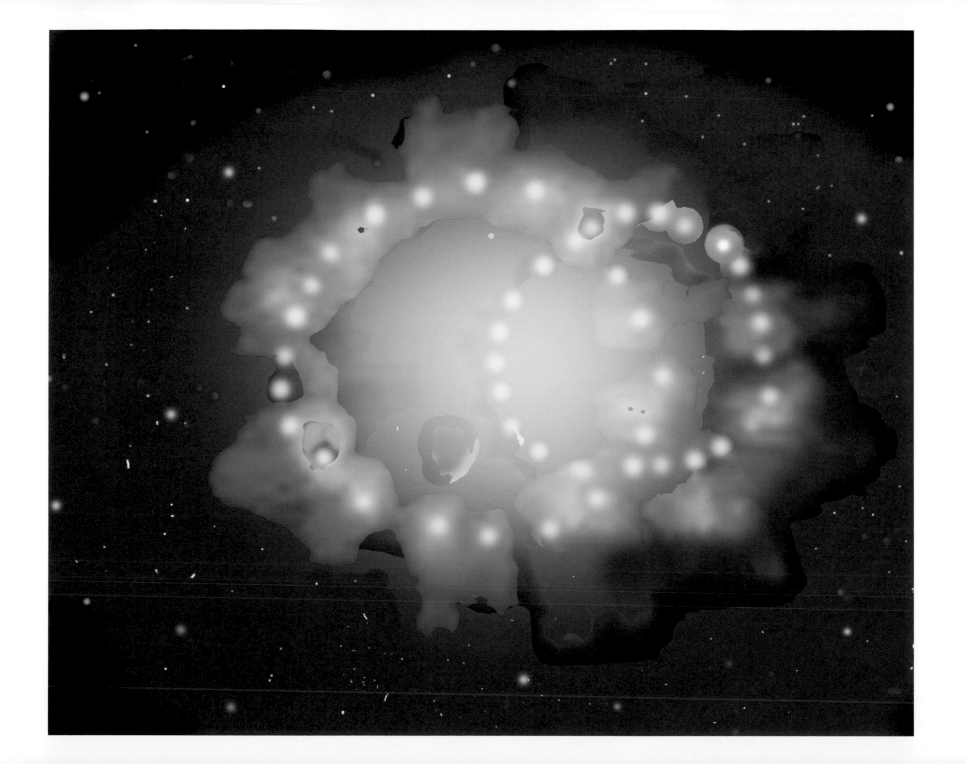

PARADISO XXXIII *46–48, 52–66*

As I drew nearer to the end of all desire,

I brought my longing's ardor to a final height,

Just as I ought. My vision, becoming pure,

Entered more and more the beam of that high light

That shines on its own truth. From then, my seeing

Became too large for speech, which fails at a sight

Beyond all boundaries, at memory's undoing—

As when the dreamer sees and after the dream

The passion endures, imprinted on his being

Though he can't recall the rest. I am the same:

Inside my heart, although my vision is almost

Entirely faded, droplets of its sweetness come

The way the sun dissolves the snow's crust—

The way, in the wind that stirred the light leaves,

The oracle that the Sibyl wrote was lost.

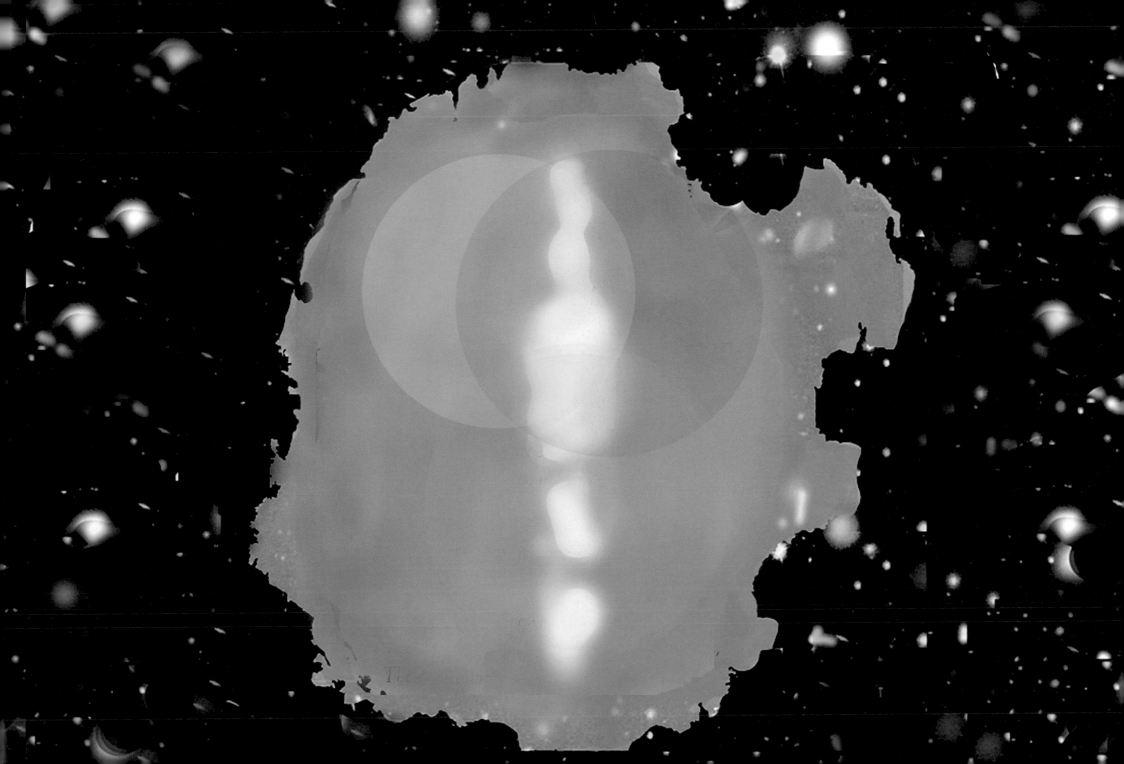

ON THE IMAGES

THIS IS MY FOURTH SERIES OF IMAGES AFTER DANTE. I have been working on the *Divine Comedy* on and off for fifty years. I made a set of thirty-five black-and-white monotypes in 1993, as illustrations for Robert Pinsky's remarkable verse translation, *The Inferno of Dante,* published by Farrar, Straus and Giroux. In 2000—sometimes adapting subjects or motifs from those monotype illustrations—I completed a suite of forty-one etchings from *Inferno.* The etchings led to a portfolio of broadsides in 2008, including images from *Purgatorio* and *Paradiso* as well as new Inferno images, with new translations by Robert Pinsky of suitable brief passages as captions. This book is based on those broadsides, (much expanded), with Robert's caption-translations. To read his *Inferno* aloud is to hear in its music Dante's sadness and awe at the way Dante's sinners harm themselves by harming others. In the English cadences, you hear the character Dante's voice of alarm, in tandem with Virgil's voice of reason.

Much of the *Inferno* is conversation, almost as if the characters are reading the poem to us. However, it is the startling and transcendent passages of description that give meat to the illustrator. The passages from *Purgatorio* and *Paradiso* I have asked Robert to provide are essentially visual, though of course charged with spiritual drama..

Why Dante? *The Divine Comedy* is regarded by many, including me, as the greatest poem ever to come out of Western Europe. It is essential reading, translated into nearly every language and illustrated by artists everywhere. My fascination with it, like that of many artists, is its evocative imagery: many a scene in the *Commedia* is hard to pass by without trying to draw it. The more time I spent reading and drawing studies, the more I realized that in the many-layered Inferno, horror is part of a complex surface interpenetrated by sorrow. Often, Dante the Pilgrim, recognizing a friend or enemy, emphasizes the person's humanity. These characters have a more distinct, palpable reality than Dante's saints. The gossipy nature of their conversation evokes the actual streets and houses of Florence.

I have illustrated a few other texts during my career, including Richard Howard's translation of Chalres Baudelaire's *Les Fleur du Mal* for publisher David R. Godine, as well as various smaller projects. These projects were, for me, more like embellishments—Howard called them "adornments"—in the tradition of the fine illustrated [or artist's] books published by Ambroise Vollard in the late nineteenth and early twentieth centuries; these editions commissioned illustrations by Bonnard, Picasso, and others, and employed exquisite fonts and high-quality paper and bindings. My engagement with Dante has been on a different scale, and of a different kind.

Illustration, like translation, is risky business. At worst, illustrations can sidetrack the reader by introducing ideas or images that change the meaning of the text, skew its tone, diminish its impact. At its best, though, illustration is a reinvention. Its success depends upon the quality of vision, in the widest sense of that term, in the images. Some texts are so wedded to their illustrations that it is hard to think of certain characters without those images in mind. Sir John Tenniel's illustrations for Lewis Carroll's *Alice's Adventures in Wonderland* come to mind, as do Édouard Manet's for

Poe's *The Raven*. The *Commedia,* in an opposite way, has a long tradition of many different illustrations, and visual responses by great artists.

Robert Pinsky and I have worked together on Dante since 1992. We have been asked many times if we intended to translate and illustrate the entire other two sections of the *Divine Comedy.* Neither of us wanted to. For my part, I was never sure I was the right artist for all three. I once thought, after completing the *Inferno* monotypes, that a group of three artists, each with specific qualities and interests, might do the ultimate contemporary illustrations for the *Commedia,* perhaps in collaboration with three poets. When—contrary to that notion—I began to work with the other two sections of the poem, I found myself responding, not to every canto, but to a few that inspired images. These images as I conceived them demanded color: for *Purgatory,* the colors of the earth, and for *Paradise,* a kind of ecstatically enhanced geometry. The superb medieval illuminations of Giovanni di Paolo are among my favorites.

This book is a fragment not only of the poem, but of its meaning. These images (and the captions kindly supplied by Robert Pinsky) are themselves fragments, and make no further claims, except as works of art. They can, in their own terms, only hint at the richness and excitement of the *Commedia*.

Michael Mazur
Cambridge, MA
2009